DINOSAUR TRACING BOOK

Trace & Color

Trace & Color

Trace & Color

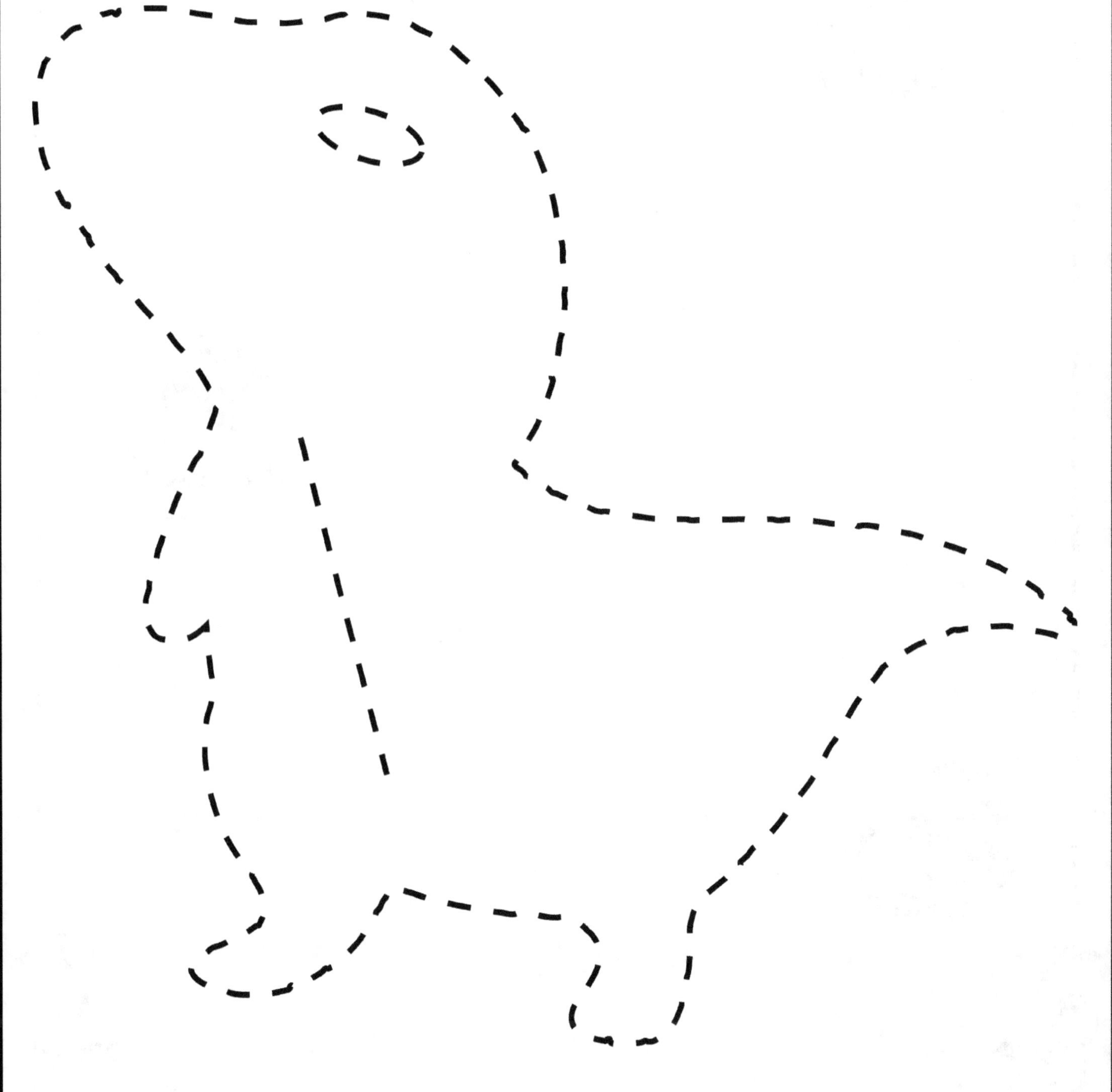

Trace & Color

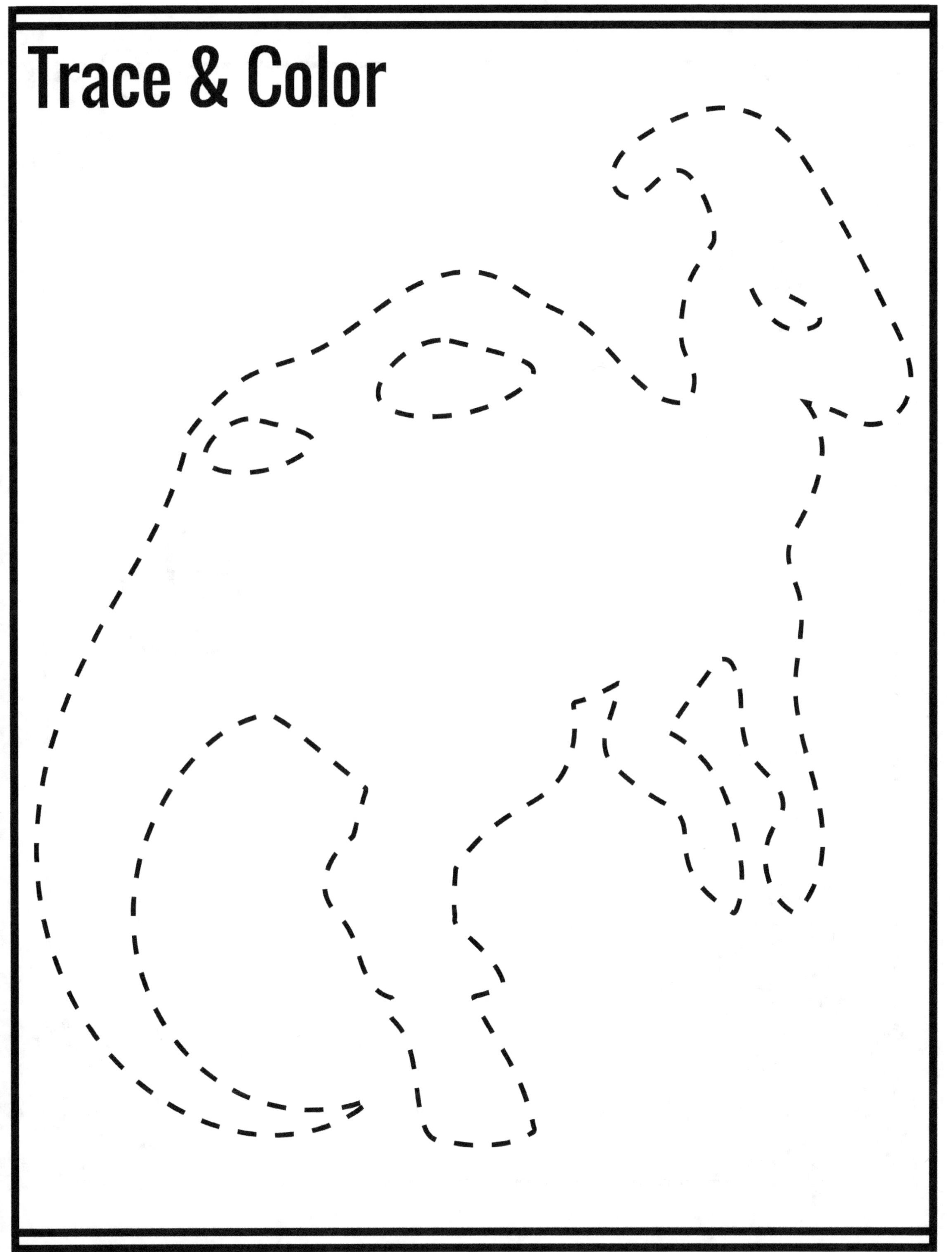

Trace & Color

Trace & Color

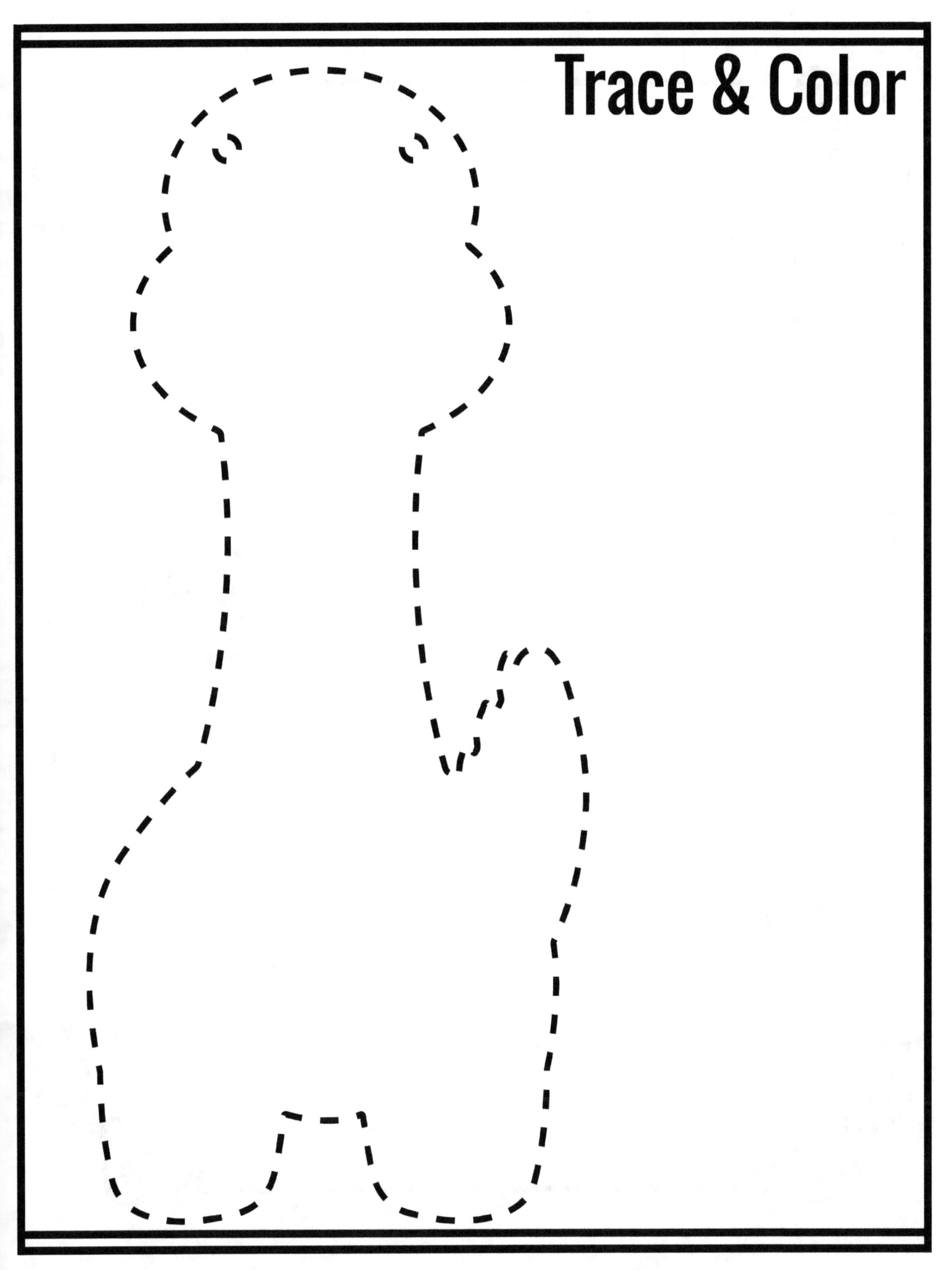
Trace & Color

Trace & Color

Trace & Color

Trace & Color

Trace & Color

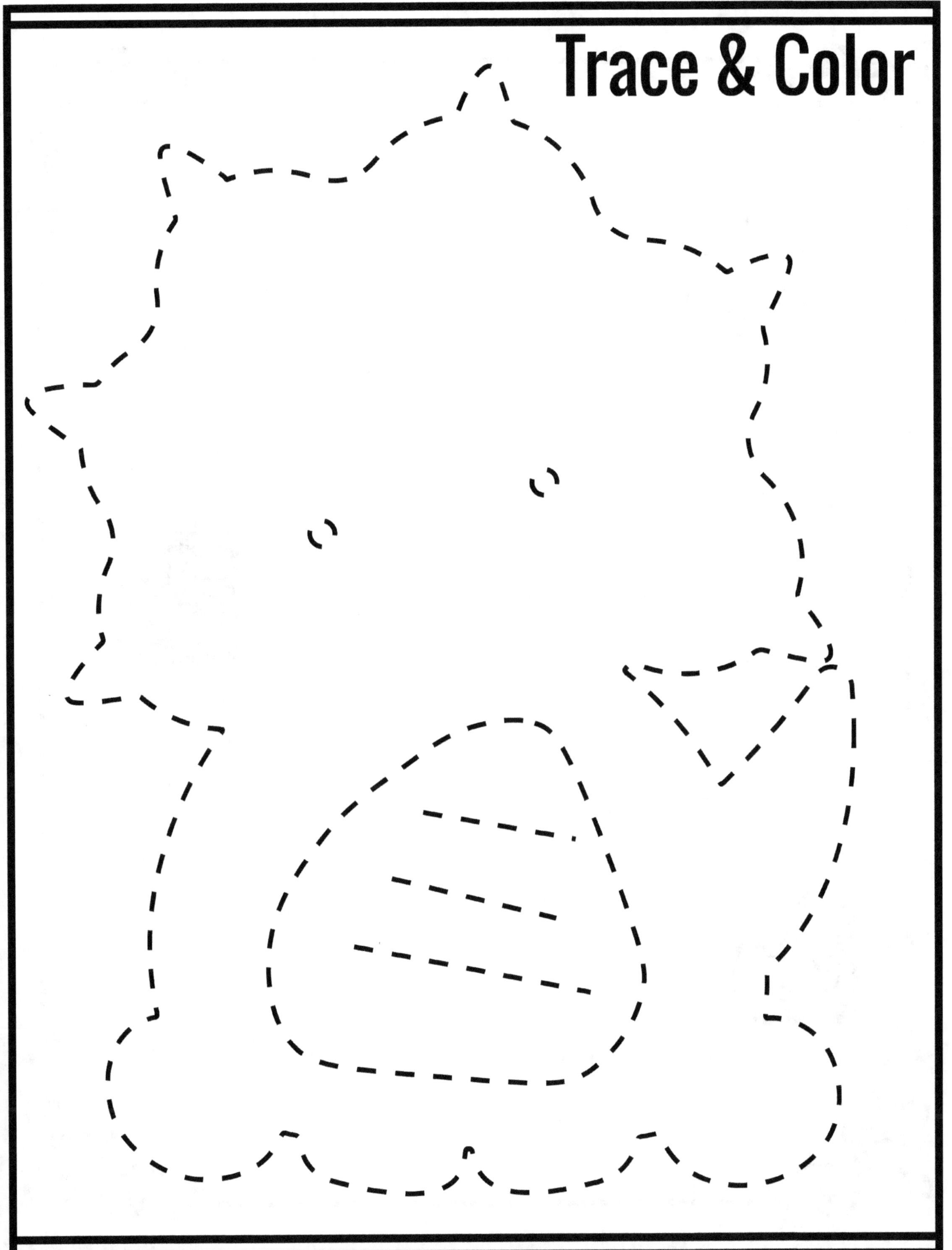

Trace & Color

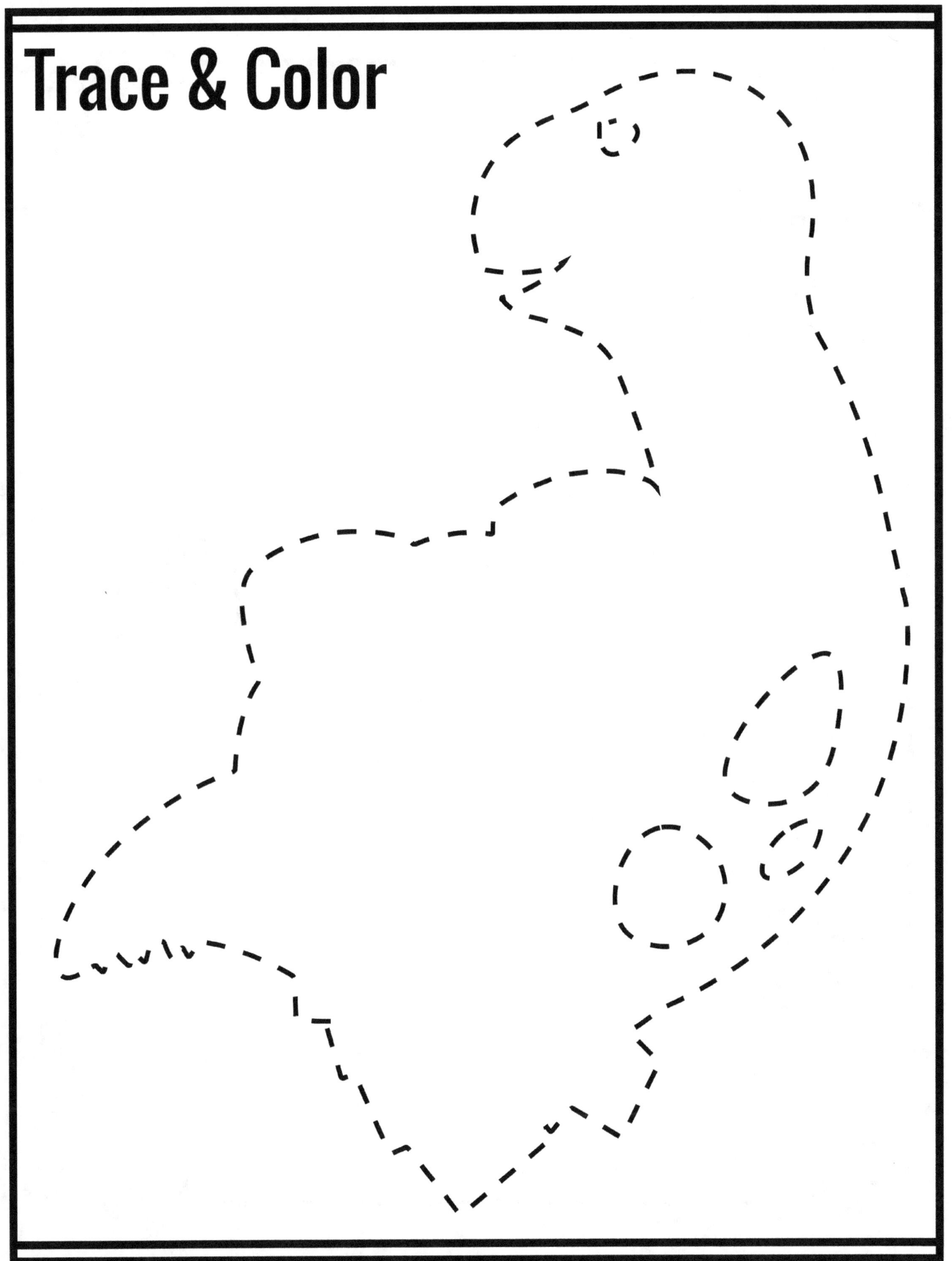

Trace & Color

www.ingramcontent.com/pod-product-compliance
Lightning Source LLC
LaVergne TN
LVHW080600160826
845677LV00010B/1936
* 9 7 9 8 4 1 4 2 4 8 0 2 6 *